Pomeranian Pandemonium
∾ and other poems ∾

Wallace B. McCall
"Poet Lawreate"

For Campbell, Caroline, Daisy, and Liam

Love, Papa

Contents

Animals

Pomeranian Pandemonium

∽◡◡∽

If you move to west Montana, you'll find living there is hard,
And death is just as random as the turning of a card.
It's wide, high desert country that's as dry as weathered bones
That lay scattered in the sage brush with the tumbleweeds
    and stones.
The winter wind will freeze your soul; the sun will boil blood.
The melting snow and pelting rain churn dirt to sucking mud.
Large predators will eat you if they catch you unawares:
Coyotes, wolves, and lions; vicious black and grizzly bears.
But the greatest danger out there in this whole wild western
    scene,
Lives lurking in a trailer in a town they named Sixteen.
It's kind of like a ghost town, if you leave you don't come back,
But there lives Bill McDonald and his Pomeranian pack.
At last count, he had fifty-two, but no one knows for sure,
Since their bloodlines and genetics are a little bit obscure.
There's one thing that's for certain, they are not to be ignored,
'Cause these furry little vermin are a vile, bloodthirsty horde.
They devour living creatures like piranha do in streams,
And while tearing tiny mouthfuls they ignore their
    victim's screams
Until at last there's silence save their panting little lungs
And the licking of their whiskers with their pinkish
    little tongues.
Now right by downtown Sixteen there's a four strand barbed
    wire fence
With a gate that Bill's chained up and locked without much
    common sense
Since no one ever goes there unless they've got the right
To hunt or graze their cattle, which is pretty black and white.
One time in late November when we'd gone out there to hunt,
We had to drive by Sixteen, and to be completely blunt,
I felt the terror building with a churning in my guts

11

When I thought about a face off with Bill's mob of manic mutts.
Maybe it was destiny or maybe it was fate,
But Walter drew the short straw so he had to get the gate.
He bolted from the truck door with the key clutched in his fist
When he heard the first crescendo through the early morning
    mist.
A furry wave advancing; a tsunami at full flood.
The canine avalanche advanced fueled by its lust for blood.
When charging at full throttle, all amassed for its attack,
There is nothing more ferocious than a Pomeranian pack.
We really thought he'd make it, that he wouldn't have a scratch,
But that moment's hesitation when he fumbled with the latch
Gave the alpha male an opening, sharp teeth caught
    woolen cuff;
Then half a hundred more piled on, and things got really rough.
Gilbert muttered softly in his heavy Southern drawl,
"Now isn't that some friggin' shit and everything and all."
We knew we couldn't help him. We figured he was done,
When suddenly behind us, the explosion of a gun.
And there stood Bill McDonald with his trusty forty-four,
Who had arrived there just in time to even up the score.
When we expressed our gratitude, Bill looked us in the eye,
"I don't know why you'd thank me. I was aimin' fer the guy!"

Makin' Bacon

My wife called me at half past five.
Said, "We are trapped like bees in a hive,
By wild hogs ruttin' in our front yard.

"A big, black boar and a spotted sow
Have both been at it six hours now.
Our back door's locked and the front door's barred.

"They're lootin', rootin', raisin' Hell.
They're gruntin', squealin', startin' to smell.
The dog is barkin', pitchin' a fit.

"That boar's got tusks like a buffalo horn.
The lawn's so plowed we might plant corn.
I sure ain't happy, not one damned bit!"

I fired her up and hit the street.
Pulled my .357 from under my seat.
I hate to hear that my dog's upset.

There they were by the driveway's fork,
Five Hundred pounds of impassioned pork.
I grabbed my gun and began to sweat.

Hot and humid in mid July.
In my Gucci shoes and paisley tie,
I was more than slightly overdressed.

He popped his chops and seemed to grin.
His eyes were as black and as cold as sin.
I'd have to say that I was impressed.

The boar hog swaggered down our lane,
The lust expunged from his porcine brain.
The sow took off by a different route.

Our yard's enclosed by hogwire fence,
That we had installed at great expense,
To keep our pets in and critters out.

She tore off like a scalded fool,
'Cross the wooden deck by the swimming pool,
With me behind her in hot pursuit.

Round and round like a mid-town trolly,
Here comes the pig; then here comes Wally.
I knew in my heart I couldn't shoot.

I got a rope from off the tree
Where we hook the dog when she has to pee.
Then in the end, I quickly tied a noose.

I thought a lasso'd do the job,
And I'd hogtie her like Cowboy Bob,
'Cause we both were running out of juice.

A few more laps around we go'd,
But it was clear that our pace had slowed.
She was lathered up and so was I.

Just when I think this pig's real dumb
She headed on out the way she'd come.
I raised my hand and fondly waved goodbye.

I'd been at it over an hour.
I said I'd need a nice, cold shower.
My wife smiled and said that she'd agree.

'Cause after those lascivious swine
Had spent that day all intertwined,
In front of her...Well, buddy, so did she.

Manatee Matinee

We attended our first manatee matinee;
It was sort of a maritime bovine ballet.
Their cleft whiskered lips were all bristled and spiney
And bubbles of gas would erupt from their hiney.
Two paddley flippers, a fan for a tail
Propelled them sedately, both he and female.
Full figured, rotunded, prodigious, obese;
Their demeanor's demure; they're serenely at peace,
'Til some operator of jet ski or boat
Roars over their backs as they placidly float,
Marking brands on their hides with the prop or the keel,
Lacerated abrasions that never quite heal.
It's hard to imagine that sailors of yore
When they happened upon our subtropical shore,
That due to poor eyesight or dense morning fog,
Or perhaps after drinking their ration of grog,
Came then to believe or perhaps just to wish,
That the top half was woman, the bottom half fish!
The mermaid's a myth they say dwells in the sea,
But she's been well disguised as the poor manatee.

Animal Rights

One day, God's creatures, great and small,
Decided they had taken all
That they could take without amends
From greedy *Homo sapiens*.
They'd carried loads and given rides;
Donated milk and meat and hides;
Been sliced and diced, ground up, deboned.
They tested drugs. They'd now been cloned.
How many more would be devoured
Before they got themselves empowered?

Some zoologic Ph.D.'s,
With funds from federal agencies,
Experimented to detect
Which species had the intellect
To go to court and wage some fights
Asserting animalistic rights—
Equal Protection Under Law.
They'd wage the battle tooth and claw
Until at last they'd be set free
From their domestic husbandry.

They inventoried strengths and faults,
Then analyzed the test results
For humanistic attributes
More prominent in certain brutes
Than others (like invertebrates,
And fish and eels and sharks and skates).
They picked emotions and intent,
Self-consciousness, intelligent,
Communicative skills to talk
By bellow, grunt, or squeak or squawk.

Their spokesman was a Parrot Gray,
Articulate in every way.
Four primate species they have chose:
Orangutans and bonobos,
Gorillas and the chimpanzees.
The long shot pick was bumblebees.
The dolphin and the elephant
And man's best friend, the dog, they want.
This plaintiff class was set to sue,
But don't you know that trouble'd brew?

The lions, so-called King of Beasts,
Decided they'd be making feasts
Of anyone who seemed inclined
To keep the group thus un-felined.
Marsupials would not forgive.
They had no representative.
The avians and insects bitched
Demanding everything be switched
To ratios of specie size.
The primates smiled and rolled their eyes.

A Bill of Rights, their master plan
Resembling the one for man
Was lobbied loud and long by troops
From varied special interest groups.
The canines whined the major thrust
Should simply be, "In Dog We Trust."
The worker bees sought rights to pay.
The dolphins wanted rights to play.
The parrots shouted, "Freedom! Speech!"
The primates opted not to preach.

Prolonged debate for days and nights
Resulted in their Bill of Rights.
No animal shall be consumed.
No bird shall ever be deplumed.
No humanoid shall ever wear
A coat of hide or pelt of hair.

Domesticated fowl get paid
For every single egg that's laid.
There would be no hunting season;
Not again, for any reason.

No more teaching stupid tricks,
Like playing dead, retrieving sticks.
No more experiments on rats
Or guinea pigs or dogs or cats.
A ban on all insecticides.
No more free horse and pony rides.
And then the primates slipped one past
Amended at the very last:
No right, no rule, and no decree
Was good unless the apes agree.

Their pressure point from this day hence
Was civil disobedience.
Domestic stock would go on strike.
The farmers all could take a hike.
There'd be no eggs, no milk, no cheese.
No honey from the honey bees.
The elephants would blockade roads.
The dogs would use more subtle modes,
Like soiling oriental rugs
And bringing home fleas, ticks, and bugs.

They'd boycott circuses and zoos.
They'd lie around all day and snooze,
Except to picket butcher shops
To protest sales of steaks and chops.
The birds would join in bombing runs
On fresh washed cars 'neath baking suns.
But if their pacifistic tact
Should fail to make the humans act,
They'd do whate're it took, pray tell,
To make their lives a living hell.

The bumblebees, with humming wings,
Delivered kamikaze stings.
Skunks volunteered to do their share;
Held sit ins where they fouled the air.
The porcupines launched clouds of quills
And vampire bats caused warm blood spills.
Pit vipers, buzzing, poised to strike
To demonstrate their deep dislike
Of anyone or thing that might
Oppose them in this noble fight.

Then lawyers sued in every court
For damages for every tort.
From coast to coast and state to state,
They thus commenced to litigate.
Inhumane acts must be enjoined
With punishment for rights purloined.
And Congress should correct these flaws
With Animal Protection Laws.
Then one fine day, they got it done.
The word went out, "We won! We won!"

Won what? Won what? Give us the facts!
We've won the right to pay some tax,
To pay some tolls, to pay some fees.
(Except for apes like chimpanzees.)
We won the right to live by rules
Enacted by elected fools,
Who supervise and regulate,
Bureaucratize, administrate
Their convoluted social plans.
(Exception: apes, orangutans.)

A forty-hour week of work
Applied to all with just one quirk.
The primate males would be excused.
It seems their brains were overused
Deciding what would be the best
For everyone. (They smirked in jest.)

Then, overcome by power lust,
They ruled that all the others must
Pay all the apes and bonobos
Like corporation CEOs.

And that was when things fell apart.
The lesser beasts said, "We ain't smart
Like big gorillas, chimpanzees.
From what we hears and what we sees,
It's damned unfair. It irritates.
It's prejudiced. Discriminates.
We ain't got rights. Apes took 'em all,
From God's own creatures, great and small.
We know you think we ain't got class.
You hairy apes can kiss our ass!"

Things went back like they were before.
Pastoral peace, not civil war.
The natural laws that had evolved
Still worked to get their problems solved.
They lived by seasons, stars, and moon;
The sun at dawn, at dusk, at noon;
The weather, tides, magnetic poles
Determined their respective roles.
Without their "rights," they'd been set free,
As Nature planned for them to be.

Top Dog

The dog was such a scoundrel, a misfit, and a tramp.
He'd learned his table manners living in some hobo camp.
He didn't like the winter 'cause he couldn't stand the snow,
So he hopped aboard a box car bound for San Antonio.

His coat was kind of dirty white with scattered brownish spots.
They looked more like big splotches than they did like
    polka dots.
His size you'd say was medium; his tail curled in an arc.
His voice was quite abrasive, an obnoxious, yappy bark.

His left ear stood up straight and tall; his right hung
    limply down.
His left eye was a pale sky blue; the right one, chocolate brown.
At night if you would shine a light reflecting on his head,
His brown eye shown a ghostly green; his blue one glowed
    bright red.

The little girl who found him thought he was a charming chap.
He wagged his tail, then licked her face, and climbed up in
    her lap.
She said, "I'll call him Eddie!" Then she took him home
    with her.
She didn't know that she'd been conned by such a lowly cur.

He couldn't be house broken and he soiled all the rugs.
The furniture infested with assorted fleas and bugs.
He chewed up shoes and scratched the paint by pawing at
    the doors.
His claws were gouging furrows in the shiny, hardwood floors.

He stayed in constant trouble, but what finally took the cake,
Was his jumping on the counter where he ate their sirloin
steak.
The little girl cried buckets but her father only frowned,
Then loaded up poor Eddie and he dropped him at the pound.

The other dogs could only drool and stare with mouths agape
As Eddie went to work and engineered the great escape.
He took off running toward her house when he had cleared
the   fence.
He knew that there was trouble; it was something he
could sense.

He smelled the smoke two blocks away and speeded up
his pace.
He saw that flames were flickering above the attic space.
The picture window shattered as he leaped with all his might,
Then he raced upstairs to save them from their deadly
certain plight.

Now Eddie prances proudly when she walks him to admire
His statue cast in bronze that sits atop the marble spire.
The plaque says he's a hero who is very strong and brave.
It's signed, "With love, The family you risked your life to save."

Beethoven

Beethoven the mule is nobody's fool;
He's big and he's strong, and he's smart.
His hooves are rock hard. He's held with regard,
For his super-sized helping of heart.

That day in the rain, he broke his lead chain,
And followed us out on the hunt.
"Don't care if they mind. Won't be left behind,"
He sneered with a guttural grunt.

The royal elk bull had his hands right full,
With several lascivious cows.
It raised up his ire if they should desire
To mate with some stud they'd arouse.

Young Casey cut loose a sensual ruse
Of sexual wails, moans, and mews.
He played his cow call and gave it his all,
Like a saxophone crying the blues.

The bull feel in love, like hands with a glove,
Then started to bugle his lust.
He fatally learned, 'tis best to be spurned,
For a harlot you never can trust.

He dropped as night fell, down deep in a dell.
We marveled as he lay in state.
He weighed a half ton. I lowered my gun,
Amazed at his size and his weight.

It started to snow. The problem, you know,
Was getting that bull back to camp.
The snow came down hard, as slipp'ry as lard;
The cold caused my muscles to cramp.

We sawed and we hacked; we chopped and we whacked;
We cut and we cussed in the black.
The hours went by as we rendered the guy
Into quarters, a cape, and the rack.

Past midnight it took. The ground had the look
Of the scene of a violent crime.
We next had to pack the meat on the back
Of the mules for a two-hour climb.

We staggered and fell. An icy cold Hell,
With aching and pain in each knee.
When we lost the trail in the fog and the hail,
I was feeling like poor Sam McGee.

I moaned, "If I die, I don't want to fly.
Air Rescue can save on the fuel.
Let me rigor morts, bent over of sorts,
Packed out on Beethoven the mule."

Protolofish

Most tropical fish on Caribbean shoals
When danger approaches will jump into holes
In the reef, or the rocks, or the coral that's around;
Or, absent such cover, they'll bore in the ground.

But one little fellow (whose name I forget),
Has come up with a game plan that I will just bet,
You'd never have thought of in one million years;
No matter the depth and the breadth of your fears.

These cute little fishes, the lads and the lasses,
Spend their days on their heads imitating sea grasses.
When peril's presented, these guys cease their slumber
And jump up the ass of a large sea cucumber.

While hideouts like this would most certainly pain us,
These fish head tail first up the cucumber's anus.
It's hard to explain and it's hard to respect 'em
But they're safe and secure up the cucumber's rectum.

They loll all around in abdominal gas,
Then expel themselves out once the predators pass.
The scientists say that this conduct's exotic.
I happen to think the cuke's anal erotic.

Vulture Culture

Spiraling upward on currents of air
As if they ascend an invisible stair,
Soaring the Heavens in effortless flight.
Harness the wind beneath wings open wide,
Tilting and turning they silently glide,
Drifting on currents 'til they're out of sight.

Then an aroma that wafts on the breeze
Pungent and putrid like Limburger cheese,
Titillates sensors, olfactory nerved.
Gastric temptations from morbid decay.
Something sprawls dead and is rotting away.
Hordes dropping in. It's time dinner is served.

Puree of possum. A rack of raccoon.
Disemboweled dogs causing vultures to swoon.
Rank and revolting. Disgustingly gross.
Thrusting their heads inside liver and lungs,
Smacking their beaks while they're lolling their tongues,
Mauling and brawling, they huddle in close.

Gorging with gusto. An orgy divine.
Carcass picked clean from the ribs to the spine.
Recycle experts. Waste management pros.
Dressed in dark plumage with featherless head;
Final pallbearers of that which is dead.
In through their tops out their bottoms it goes.

Climber First Timer

∽∿∾

"Go get yourself a climber," said my buddy, Buddy Blount.
"I swear to God it is the only way a man should hunt.
Forget about the ladder stands. Them tripods weigh a ton.
Go get yourself a climber and I'll show you how it's done."
The next time I was home alone, with just me and the dog,
I started flipping through Cabela's Master Catalog.
The one I bought was pricey. It really set me back.
But when it comes to climbing trees, I want the Cadillac.
One platform is the foot rest; the other is the seat;
Two cables hold them to the trunk; you strap one to
        your feet.
First lift your arms, then press down. Now lift with
        bended knee.
It's kind of like an inch worm doing pushups on a tree.
It takes a little practice and it's hard to get the knack,
Unless you've been a lineman or, perhaps, a lumberjack.
But with some trial and error, I was master of the stunt,
And expressed appreciation to my buddy, Buddy Blount.
The first day of the season, filled with joy, without a care,
Swaying gently in the breezes cantilevered in the air,
Snacking on some salted peanuts, sipping on a Mountain
        Dew,
I was peaceful as the panda I'd watched snoozing at the zoo.

The hogs showed up at five o'clock. I swear they came
        in waves.
They ripped and tore the ground apart like excavated
        graves.
One coal black boar would have to weigh, I'd guess, three
        hundred pounds.
His tusks were like stilettos and they made weird
        gnashing sounds.
In retrospect, I must confess, it wasn't very bright

27

To toss the pigs the peanuts just to watch them shove
    and fight
For the tasty little goobers that were falling from the skies.
And then the black boar got involved and I got compromised.
Coiled far below me was the tail end of the line
That I'd used to haul my gun up once I'd fastened to
    the pine,
And all that I can figure is it formed a kind of noose
By which the boar got hogtied on one leg, but three
    were loose.
He bolted like a bronco and when he reached its length
I really wished I'd bought some rope with lower tensile
    strength.
The tree was whipping wildly, it was bending to and fro.
My rifle catapulted to the plowed-up earth below.
In frantic desperation, I went searching for my knife,
But guess what I'd forgotten for the first time in my life?
We were locked up in a standoff that neither one could win,
And thus the endless siege began as darkness settled in.
The night was long and cold and wet. Mosquitoes on
    a spree,
While I sat huddled anxiously in hopes they'd rescue me.
The boar would stir and would concur by uttering a grunt
With every name that I defamed my buddy, Buddy Blount.

People

The Gator Hunter's Momma

She drives down to the boat ramp every night at half past dark
Then pulls into a vacant space where empty trailers park.
She chain smokes filtered cigarettes and rolls her window down.
She sits and swats mosquitoes with her face etched in a frown.
Her supply of Dr. Pepper's in a cooler at her feet
And country songs are playing from the boom box on her seat.
Her sad eyes search the darkness for a light approaching shore,
While her ears are tuned to listen for an airboat's distant roar.
Her boy's a gator hunter. It's his passion and his pride.
But the gator hunter's momma's feeling empty deep inside.

He was her only baby. As a kid he loved to romp
Barefooted with his beagle through the dismal cypress swamp;
Until the day the gator pulled his dog beneath the slime
And he swore an oath to get revenge until the end of time.
His airboat crushes sawgrass while careening through the night,
Red eyes reflecting brightly in his headlamp's beam of light.
His foot's jammed on the throttle; his revolver's on his hip,
With a pinch of Copenhagen tucked away behind his lip.
His harpoon flashes downward with a float tied to its cord,
Then his bangstick does its business and the gator's dragged aboard.

A fourteen-foot bull gator, prehistoric dinosaur,
Was bellowing a challenge to commence reptilian war.
The gator hunter spied him and decided it was fate
That brought them both together to expunge his soul of hate.
The capsized, sunken airboat was discovered in the grass
By two fishermen bait casting for some Okeechobee bass.
The wood harpoon was shattered and the rope was snapped like thread,
So the coroner concluded that the hunter must be dead.
His momma keeps her vigil. It's her passion and her pride.
But the gator hunter's momma's feeling empty deep inside.

31

The Bionic Cryonic

His very essence of existence was a scientific prank.
The egg from anonymity; the sperm was from a bank.
The site of his conception was a laboratory tube,
And his chromosomes were jumbled—a genetic Rubik's Cube.

The egg was then implanted in some surrogated womb,
Where its cells commenced dividing in the dark placental gloom.
On the day of his delivery, into the world he burst.
It was by Cesarean section. (He was headed out feet first.)

He never found a job he liked. He never liked to play.
His favorite food was oatmeal and his favorite color, gray.
He had no coordination and detested every sport.
He had no imagination upon which he could resort.

Never tried his hand at living, so he never learned to live.
Never gave a thought to giving so he never learned to give.
He never, ever fell in love. He never had a plan.
He knew some day he'd die alone, a boring, bitter man.

His life a total failure, he was sure that he was doomed
To spend all of his eternity where e'er he was entombed.
But then he read an article about some baseball great
Who had his body frozen to attempt to change his fate.

He, too, could be suspended for a hundred years or more,
When maybe science would progress to even up the score!
He'd have his head transplanted to a muscular physique,
And have his brain cells all enhanced by some unknown technique.

It cost him his life savings, but he didn't feel deprived,
'Cause they promised him in writing that some day he'd be revived.
With the help of cryogenics he would prove he's not a boob,
And instead of passing dust to dust, he passed from tube to tube.

Jersey Joe

∾◡◠

I'd been tending bar at Barney's for my fifteen sober years,
Dispensing high-grade alcohol and draft imported beers.
I would have sworn I'd seen it all; heard every tale of woe,
'Til that night in mid September when I served poor Jersey Joe.
His greasy hair was curly and disheveled on his head.
His rheumy eyes were bloodshot and his bulbous nose glowed red.
His skin all pale and pasty like he'd never seen the light,
And the bags beneath his lower lids were darker than the night.
His teeth were stained with nicotine. His tie hung on a clip.
A Camel with no filter clung on limply to his lip.
Joe's voice was coarse and raspy, like a creaky rusty hinge
When he ordered scotch and soda to commence his nightly binge.
Joe hunkered on the bar stool by a clean cut guy named Jon,
Who had asked to find the channel that the Gator game was on.
We'd been watching Tebow lead his team to yet another romp
Of some SEC opponent that had ventured to The Swamp.
"I should'a won the goddamn thing. The whole damn ball'a wax.
I thought the guy was bluffin' and I was holdin' jacks.
So when he gave that smart ass smile and pushed his chips all in,
I said, 'That stupid bastard's gonna take it on the chin!'
Then the scrawny, little asshole in his cowboy hat and jeans,
He takes the pot and kills me with a pair'a friggin' queens!"
The football game forgotten, we had found a better show
As we listened to the diatribe spew forth from Jersey Joe.
He paused to order dinner then we watched in disbelief
As he attacked, with knife and fork, a slab of rare roast beef.
First off he cut it lengthwise then next he turned his plate
And slashed three times across it. (It was more like lacerate.)
He thrust a dripping hunk of meat into his gaping maw
Then began to desecrate it with his grizzled lower jaw.
A steady stream of expletives were liberally dispersed
With numerous examples of just how his luck was cursed.
"My fathuh's got the cansuh…," then Joe made a choking sound.

33

His face turned bluish purple and his eyes got big and round.
Then just when I thought Jersey Joe would hear the angels sing,
Big Jon the Gator grabbed him and he did the Heimlich thing.
When Joe resumed his gnawing and had swallowed what he'd chewed,
We all expected he'd express his solemn gratitude.
But Jersey Joe stayed focused and he never missed a beat,
"My fathuh's got the cansuh…," as he stabbed a hunk of meat.

The Outfitter

∽∾∿

We found him on the Internet through "elk" and "Idaho."
His rates were fair, but still and all, we're talking major dough.
He sounded young but honest when we called him on his cell,
So we wrote the check and mailed it. We decided, "What the hell.
We hope he's not a drunkard or a liar or a fake,
But we won't know 'til we meet him if we've made a big mistake."

He had some reservations that just would not dissipate:
Two middle-aged flatlanders from the so-called Sunshine State?
A lawyer and some guy who claimed he owned a hardware store?
These two would be complaining when they first got saddle sore.
They couldn't climb the mountains and they couldn't breathe the air.
He bet he'd earn his money when he babysat this pair.

When finally we met up we all checked each other out,
And in each others' faces we could read concern and doubt.
"They're just some frigging cowboys and they sure look tough and mean."
I had a sinking feeling somewhere down around my spleen.
"A couple city slickers from the East," they thought with dread.
"Before this thing is over we'll bet one of them is dead."

They showed us how to load the mules explaining all the tack.
We rode and climbed through rain and snow and never once turned back.
We camped in comfort. Slept on cots in four walled canvas tents.
The stock grazed, hobbled out at night with no corral or fence.
We cowboyed up the steepest trail they call The Beaver Slide.
They told us, "If he's going down, jump to the uphill side."

We trusted them. They trusted us. A bond began to grow.
We had a drink and shared our lives while watching embers glow.
When it was time to say goodbye, I didn't want to leave,

But we had our commitments made with no chance for reprieve.
He shook my hand, looked in my eyes and smiled, "I don't know when,
But I sure hope before too long, our trails will cross again."

The Bingo Binger

You'd find her every evening at a different lodge or hall
Where she'd feel her pulse accelerate when they began to call
The letters and the numbers that were flashed up on the board,
Then she'd mutter her "Hail Mary's" and she'd pray, "Please help me, Lord."
A sterling silver crucifix for luck clenched in her fist,
Which, when she had a winning card, she reverently kissed.
She claimed it was her hobby and it wasn't "nothin' more."
"Well, maybe it's my passion, but I can quit," she swore.

She named their children Ben and Ivan, Nathan, George, and Otis.
Whereupon her spouse woke up and suddenly took notice
That perhaps what he'd considered just a trifling affliction
Was actually a catastrophic gambling addiction.
She finally tried the Twelve Steps of the Bingoers Anon,
But was bored by weekly meetings where the talk droned on and on.
Eventually she relapsed at the Elks one Tuesday night,
But she won a hundred dollars so it all turned out alright.

Then one fine day, in disbelief, her eighty-year-old eyes
Espied an advertisement for a thousand dollar prize
To a single lucky winner of a Jackpot Bingo game.
She said, "If someone's going to win, it *will* be this old dame!"
It took all her life savings, but she purchased thirty cards.
She taped them all together and they stretched out several yards.
She'd just lined up her markers, when a chill ran down her spine,
As her dreaded rival, Flossie, waddled slowly down the line.

They sat across the table and they glared each other down
Until the first ball popped up for the fateful final round.
Then as her cards filled up with blots, she knew that she could win.

Her breathing came in panting breaths as sweat dripped from her chin.
And when they called, "I–seventeen," she joyfully cried, "BING—,"
Then clutched her chest and passed out cold. It was an awful thing.
But Flossie grinned in triumph as she stole the card to show
That *she'd* won the thousand dollars when she bellowed out the "O."

The Hedonistic Evangelistic

The Very Reverend Brother Love claimed he'd been sent down from above
To found The Holy and Prophetic Evangelistic Copacetic Altruistic and Wholistic Christian
Church.

His hair blown dry and lacquered, hanging on his back a placard
Proclaiming, "It's More Blessed, Lord, to Give Than to Receive!"
But let's assure there's no mistake; when the faithful gave, he'd take.
Then he'd grant their sinful souls a brief reprieve.

There was just no way to measure all the hedonistic pleasure
That the Reverend Brother Love chose to embrace.
Imported caviar, patés, filet mignons, and crème brûlées,
While God's Glory shone about his pious face.

His buttocks, big as boulders, extended well out past his shoulders.
His physique was bleak and rather like a gourd.
He had a waddle to his gait and a sanctimonious hate
For them condemned who didn't love the Lord.

With some heavy, labored breathin', he would castigate the heathen
Who would drink and cuss and smoke and fornicate.
Every one a deadly sin, he would caution with chagrin,
As he piled another helping on his plate.

His congregation'd smile at him all decked out in style
With purple robes and golden cummerbunds.
But despite what he explained, they all looked a little pained
About the checks returned for insufficient funds.

It was really quite a shock to his unsuspecting flock.
As Lisping Larry said, he was "Thurprithed."
As long as they shall live, the thing they can't forgive,
Is the fact that Brother Love had never tithed.

Tommy's Tooth

My poor old friend, Tommy, thought he was a wimp,
That day in Palatka cast netting for shrimp.

He reared right on back and he gave it a fling,
But a lower bicuspid got caught on a string.

The net opened wide but then so did his mouth.
As the net headed north, his bicuspid flew south.

"I busted my denture," he moaned with chagrin,
As he tugged on the rope and he hauled the net in.

His cast netting buddy's the inventive sort.
"You ain't got a problem," he said with a snort.

"Come out to my workroom 'cause I've got a lot
Of tusks from wild boars that I've happened to shot."

"We'll make you a new one. It may sound uncouth,
But I'm tellin' you, Tommy, a tooth is a tooth!"

They picked out a beauty; like ivory it shone.
The drill made a hum as it sliced through the bone.

They shaped it and ground it and when they were through,
They stuck it in place with a big gob of glue.

Their dentition project took most of the night,
But the dawn soon revealed that the tooth was too white!

A pot of black coffee they put on to brew.
Tom lit up a smoke and he put in a chew.

He got kind of hyper, but gave it his best,
And in three sleepless nights it was stained like the rest.

That tooth worked out great but his wife took it hard,
On those nights that he'd sneak out and root up the yard.

Obituary Writer

∽⸲⸱∾

Your journalistic journey you expected would be brighter,
But fate dictates what we become, Obituary Writer.
Demanding daily deadlines filled your heart and mind with dread,
As you composed in written prose brief lines about the dead.
You wrote the short biographies of heroes and of grinches,
Their lifetime stories now condensed to several column inches.
A life of living color; an incandescent light;
That you must re-illuminate in only black and white.
The spirit liberated and exalted by your word,
While the body in the parlor lay in wait to be interred.
With euphemisms utilized you chronicled the way
The Dear Departed exited on Final Judgment Day.
Such subtle innuendo by which you did abide,
Like, "He died unexpectedly" when it was suicide.
Was "lengthy illness" cancer or some flu of deadly strain?
Was "suddenly" a heart attack or stroke within the brain?
Was "accident" an auto or a motorcycle crash,
Or a deadly, drunken stumble at a final birthday bash?
Each lineage and legacy, each ancestor and heir,
You dutifully recorded with a rare artistic flair.
Accomplishments; adventures; curriculum vitaes;
Chronologies and histories; prolific résumés;
They're all encapsulated in some stirring necrologues
Which you composed while comatose in alcoholic fogs.
But what will you have authored as your final paragraph?
Your last goodbye? Your adios? Eternal epitaph?
These last words you perfected. These last words all your own.
These last words you requested are engraved upon your stone:

> His by-lines
> Were 'bye lines.
> His dead lines
> Met deadlines.

Sullen Sue

She was vicious and pernicious. She was evil through and through.
Upon each breast she had engraved a scorpion tattoo.
Her hair was black as raven wings; her eyes gleamed glacial blue.
She rode a Harley chopper and they called her Sullen Sue.

She said she'd been a dancer at a high-end topless bar.
She claimed that back in Hollywood she'd been a porno star.
She'd learned her sport, she would retort, in the back seat of a car,
But injuries to both her knees left her stamina subpar.

At night she'd meet the dealers in a corner of the park,
Arranging buys for crack and coke in shadows deep and dark.
Until they'd been imprisoned in a jail cell cold and stark,
They never knew that Sullen Sue was an undercover narc.

A Song and a Smoke

She lives to hear music. It speaks to her soul.
From Motown to Nashville; the Blues, Rock and Roll.
She moves and she sways to the tunes in her head,
By Elvis; The Eagles; by Joplin; The Dead.
She sings right out loud 'cause she knows every word
To each song, you would swear, that she ever has heard.
She seems in a trance or she's under the spell
Of the beat that's pulsating each vibrating cell.
When she feels alone and her spirit is broke,
She goes to her car for a song and a smoke.
She takes a deep drag, feels the sounds fill the air,
And thinks to herself, "This is better than prayer."

Gonzague Côte

Gonzague Côte was a logger from the Province of Quebec,
A burly French Canadian who didn't have neck.
His hands were huge and calloused. If you'd ask him he'd explain
How he lost an index finger when he caught it in a chain.
His beard was black and tangled; his eyes a wrinkled squint.
His remaining teeth were off-white with a slightly greenish tint.
He'd timber in the winter when the snow was deep and hard.
He'd fell 'em; top 'em; trim 'em; then he'd haul 'em to the yard,
With his huge bay gelded Belgian that he'd strangely named Pierre,
Which he thought was rather regal and it had a certain flair.
He built a one room cabin made of logs he'd cut and sawed,
Where he lived alone all winter until the ground had thawed.
One day a hiker happened by and spied the wooden shack.
A horse was tied to the hitching post, smoke billowed from the stack.
He summoned up his courage, then knocked loudly on the door.
He heard the sound of hob nailed boots clump loudly on the floor.
"Entrez! Entrez!" yelled Gonzague. "But don' bring in da cold.
"Some day I move to Florida. Dis wedder's gettin' old."
A Homelite sat in pieces, oil dripping from the chain,
Which gave the checkered tablecloth another brownish stain.
"You like to have some breakfast, eh?" inquired the cordial host.
"I got some eggs and bacon. You like coffee? I got toast."
Into the blackened cast iron stove, he crammed another log.
He fried a slab of fatback he had butchered from his hog.
He blew away some ashes from the stove top where the bread
Was toasting, then he turned around and slowly scratched his head.
A chipped enamel basin was stacked high with dirty plates.
The silverware was scattered in a pan set on some crates.
He took a food encrusted fork and wiped it on his shirt,
Then opened up his pocket knife, inspecting it for dirt.
After slicing strips of bacon, with the bread all toasty brown,

He served it with a flourish on a plate turned upside down.
He pushed aside the chainsaw parts, "Come now, sit down and eat.
Dis cold she make you hungry, so enjoy. Bon appetite!"

Legal

Aiken Paine

∽∾∽

I had a client once whose car got run down by a train.
His name was quite appropriate. They called him Aiken Paine.

We figured he'd been drinking, but he claimed a strange attack
Of confusion'd come upon him when he parked across the track.

He said he was quite fortunate and glad to be alive,
But how'd that damned train hit him when he'd parked right in his drive?

His skull, crushed like an eggshell that had fallen on a grate,
Was bonded back together with a shiny, metal plate.

He right eye gazed at heaven and his left one at the ground,
Which made his friends uncomfortable when Aiken came around.

His jaw was pure titanium. (He favored softer food.)
It made a strangely, squeaky sound whenever Aiken chewed.

The ringing in his ears was like the bells of Notre Dame.
If you wanted his attention; well, you'd have to yell his name.

His neck was fused together so he couldn't move his head.
He'd turn around completely like a dog about to bed.

He missed his arms immensely when he had to scratch an itch.
He'd mutter softly to himself that, "Sometimes life's a bitch."

The two prosthetic legs he wore would look a little queer,
When Aiken got confused and put the feet back towards the rear.

I figured that the jury would be swayed by their emotion,
And my brilliant final argument would be a magic potion.

When it was finally over, I wept tears for Aiken Paine.
For the verdict that they rendered was in favor of the train.

The Radical Viatical

❧

"I can feel the care and kindness
That your loving hearts exude.
I can sense your sensitivity,"
The beaming salesman cooed.
"You comprehend the touchstone
Of the fundamental plan,
Formulated by our Maker
To assist our fellow man.
For those of us whom God has blessed
With fortune and with wealth,
We owe a debt to those accursed
With fatal, failing health.
I know of souls who have no joy.
Their lives are wracked by sorrow.
Their hope is for a miracle
So they can see tomorrow."
His voice was choked. He gasped for breath.
His eyes welled up with tears.
He knew his words were magic
And were music to their ears.

"I know a thirty-year-old man
Who has contracted AIDS.
He spends each day at home alone
With darkened window shades.
He's all emaciated and
He's chronically depressed.
His body's oozing open sores
'Cause it's immune suppressed.
He can't afford to buy the drugs
He needs to fight the pain.
I've never seen a sadder sight
Than poor Eugene Fontaine.

51

He's used up all his savings
To combat this dread disease,
But it's in its final stages
And has knocked him to his knees.
We do have one solution thanks
To several legal scholars.
Eugene has life insurance worth
A half a million dollars."

"Gene doesn't have a single heir,
No one he can endow.
He really needs financial help.
He'd like some money now.
His doctor's signed a letter in
Which he has certified,
That before another year has passed,
This patient will have died.
You folks can buy some happiness
For Gene's last days on earth,
To help restore his self-esteem
And give his life some worth.
Your love will send a message
Like a banner that's unfurled.
Your cash will send Gene packing
For a trip to Disney World.
The poor wretch has so much to lose,
And you so much to gain.
Now, who'll extend a helping hand
To young Eugene Fontaine?"

Two dozen eyes cast downward at
Two dozen shuffling feet.
Two dozen buttocks stuck like glue
To each one's folding seat.
The salesman played his trump card.
His time had been well spent.
"Did I mention that your earnings
Will be forty-six percent?"
Then they all rose with one accord

And fought to get in line.
The sweat from their excitement made
Their eager faces shine.
They wanted in the action.
They were anxious to invest.
But only three had ready cash
And he turned down the rest.
The salesman then departed to
Deposit his commission.
He didn't know—or didn't say—
That Gene was in remission.

These three were thus united in
Their search for sudden wealth,
Which was totally dependent
On the state of Eugene's health.
Mary Wilson was a widow
Who was morbidly obese.
She liked to chew on chocolates in
Her quest for inner peace.
Big Mike O'Leary daily drank
A quart of Bombay Gin.
He said he tried the Twelve Steps but
They nearly did him in.
Percy Lovejoy Patterson was
Very suave and slick.
He was a trust fund baby who
Had never hit a lick.
So every night all bowed their heads
And spoke to God on high.
Eugene would always pray he'd live
And they all prayed he'd die.

Eugene survived as years went by,
As healthy as a horse.
While Mary Wilson's health declined
As nature took its course.
She finally passed away one day
With hardly any mention.

She had a very fatal stroke
From chronic hypertension.
O'Leary's diabetes led
Him to hydro-nephrosis,
But his death was finally caused by
Alcohol induced cirrhosis.
Percy Lovejoy Patterson was
Hitting off the tee,
When the golf ball struck his temple
Ricocheting off a tree.
Eugene Fontaine outlived them all,
Became a wealthy man.
Investing in viaticals
Was his financial plan.

Poetic Justice

The Lawyer

Howland Hornblow was a lawyer who proclaimed it his intent
To assure that his existence was a media event.
He never met a microphone he didn't love and lust
With which he'd speak exhaustively 'til he was dry as dust.
His commercial advertisements inundated television.
His Teflon-coated ego would deflect all their derision.
To anyone who'd listen he would brag each day was crammed
With a clientele consisting of the dead, the lame, the damned.

The Doctor

Malcolm Practiss was a doctor so obsessed to cut and stitch,
He became a plastic surgeon who became extremely rich.
He never had to wait on Medicare or Medicaid
Because with plastic surgery, the patient always paid.
With gifted hands he could create an ermine from a toad,
But he seemed to have some problems when the anesthesia flowed.
When his malpractice carrier grew tired of paying claims,
The elevated premiums hurt his financial aims.

The Insurance Executive

Gready Proffitt was a businessman who knew the bottom line:
Without a profit his career would wither on the vine.
When the market took a tumble and investment income dropped,
He watched his bonus dwindle and eventually it stopped.
He knew somewhere there had to be a patsy he could name;
Some unsuspecting scapegoat or a villain he could frame.
He thus commenced to ponder and to think and cogitate
When he realized their answered prayer would be to legislate.

The Politician

Smiley Bouffant was a servant of the public so he said,
Through shiny teeth that gleamed below his perfect, blown dry head.
He vowed to voters from his heart that he could feel their pain.
His positions changed direction like an oiled weathervane.
Big donations were his lifeblood and he lived to be transfused
By soft money from an industry that knew he could be used
To manipulate the system for its own financial gain;
And the coffers overflowed for his political campaign.

The Strategy

Doctor Practiss grabbed the headlines when he organized a strike
By physicians who were voicing their dismay and their dislike
Of the premiums that they were charged to get themselves insured
Against malicious lawsuits filed by patients they had cured.
"Uneducated jurors render verdicts out of sight,
Thanks to greedy lawyers who ignore the poor physicians' plight!
There has to be some limit on this 'Lotto in the Courts,'
Or there won't be any healthcare!" they cried with indignant snorts.

The Law

The bill that Bouffant introduced was lobbied long and loud.
His stirring speeches on the floor would make his mother proud.
The law they passed put caps upon awards for things like pain
And suffering; parental care lost when a mom was slain.
No recompense for altering your normal state of mind.
No payment for the patient's eyes which have been rendered blind.
The worse you're hurt, the less you get, was how the law was framed.
By Practiss, Proffitt, Bouffant, a huge victory was claimed.

Epilogue

To thank them for their efforts, Practiss volunteered with glee
To give Bouffant a face-lift which he would perform for free;
And liposuction fat from Proffitt's most prodigious girth.
But some complications planted both of them beneath the earth.

Their grieving widows were irate and wanted much to sue.
They consulted with Old Hornblow and they asked him what to do.
He explained that he was sorry and felt bad from what he saw,
But their claims were rendered worthless since their husbands changed the law.

My Cellular Phone

Sometimes my thoughts hearken to those days of yore;
Those days that preceded; those days well before;
Those days I would quietly spend all alone;
Before they invented the cellular phone.

I'm now so important, it's critical that
Everyone knows where precisely I'm at.
And if my proximity cannot be near,
It's crucial at least that I lend them my ear.

If I'm in an airplane up flying around,
The instant I feel the wheels touching the ground,
I reach for my belt and I turn my phone on
To share where I am and how long I'll be gone.

I talk really loud so folks know how it feels
To make big decisions and close business deals.
I can tell by their stares they're in awe and agree
They are blessed to be there in the presence of me.

It's etched on the faces of those reading books,
(Who keep casting their eyes with inquisitive looks),
That they are intrigued by what I have to say;
That I have enlightened and brightened their day.

I'm always considerate, never a load.
In church it's turned on to the vibration mode.
Then when it starts buzzing, I whisper, "Excuse;"
Step over the faithful in prayer on the pews.

And unlike some people with no class at all,
Before I respond to an incoming call

In restaurants where I'm ingesting my food,
I try first to swallow whatever I've chewed.

I now can take photos, send message in text.
And God only knows what they'll come up with next.
While using the urinal, straddling the throne,
I'm getting it done with my cellular phone.

Campaign Distain

∾◡∾

The polls just closed at seven. The votes have all been cast.
Of mud that's slung
And cattle dung
We hope we've heard the last.

Commercials clogged the airways, incessant, day and night.
Inundated
Saturated
No respite from our plight.

Next day, the pharmaceuticals, the whole ungodly tribe,
For all our ills
Promoting pills
Your doctor should prescribe.

If all the politicians took the drugs as advertised
Then you and me
Would likely be
Most pleasantly surprised.

Lipitor and Plavix cure their cold and hardened hearts
Coronaries
From primaries
No longer play a part.

Prevacid stops their heartburn and Xanax calms their brains
So they resist
And don't persist
With negative campaigns.

They now can stop their restless legs, a syndrome that's no fun.
There'd be no race
To win first place
They'd lose the urge to run.

Robert L. Keele, Ph.D.

∽◡∾

Whenever you lectured, Professor Bob Keele,
(Your jaw, we supposed, manufactured from steel),
You'd discourse nonstop on distinctions to draw
From the cases that made Constitutional Law.

Our hands would be cramping. Our fingers would ache,
As page after page of note taking we'd make.
We listened transfixed to this great pedagogue,
Who gave without pausing each day's dialogue.

With Madison holding Marbury at bay,
Chief Justice John Marshall was who saved the day;
Preserving the right in the highest of courts
To settle disputes of both crimes and of torts.

The *stare decisis* we follow today
Was colored by Black, by two Whites, and a Gray.
Both Burger, Frankfurter gave us food for thought.
With Warren and Douglas, conservatives fought.

We learned of the "Equal Protectionist Clause;"
Of searches and seizures; of probable cause;
No stopping and frisking; due process of law.
On such meaty concepts you'd chew and you'd gnaw.

Expounding on freedom of speech and the press.
Extolling our rights to explain and express
Whatever opinions (no matter how vile),
But just don't yell, "Fire!" in some theater aisle.

Nardone reaped "the fruit of the poisonous tree."
The "fruit" got suppressed and Nardone got set free.
Then *Gideon* sounded the clarion call:
The right to free counsel extended to all.

61

Miranda regretted his slip of the tongue
And the long term in jail it had probably brung.
Sent back to the streets, he could crow and could strut,
'Cause he knew of his right then to keep his mouth shut.

You taught us why prayer was abolished in school;
Why Separate but Equal's no longer the rule.
Our homes should be private, protected from scorn,
(Unless we've a penchant for harder core porn).

The only Amendment they'd ever repeal,
Was Number Eighteen which they passed with such zeal,
That no one considered or bothered to think
 Of our absolute right to partake of strong drink.

Professor Bob Keele, we applaud your career.
We give you our thanks and we give you a cheer!
Enjoy your retirement with all you have got.
You at last have your freedom—unlike poor Dred Scott.

Florida

I-95

His heartburn awakes him in the still of the morn,
And he wishes to God that he'd never been born.
He pops down a Prozac to conquer his fear,
Then he swallows a Zantac he chases with beer.
He fastens his seatbelt and girds up his loins,
Backs out of his driveway and suddenly joins,
The great mobile masses who hope to survive,
Their rush hour journey on I-95.

There's harried young Suzi, her foot on the throttle,
Who mascaras eyelashes, feeding baby a bottle.
She paints on her lipstick while brushing her hair,
And peruses the want ads to hire an au pair.

A truck's spilling gravel all over the road,
Seems that Pedro, the driver, never covered his load.
But he's happily driving along dropping rocks,
That crack several windshields every couple of blocks.

Tyrone and Jerome, their hot car filled with loot,
Watch out for da po'lice who might be in pursuit.
Their radio's blaring loud rap from the 'hood,
One more V.O.P.* and they're both gone for good.

Bubba's King of the Road in his jacked pickup truck,
With the wide tractor tires he won't ever get stuck.
But, he's riding so high that he doesn't know yet,
That he's driving right over a Chevy Corvette.

There's little old Florence so blind and so frail,
That she's using the bumps between lanes to drive braille.
Her cataracts render her lenses opaque,
So for safety she drives with one foot on the brake.

The developer, Irving, in his long white Mercedes,
Organizing a tryst with professional ladies.
Yelling into his cellular, lights up a cigar,
There's a faux gold insignia on the hood of his car.

Roadhog calls Hound Dog on the trucker's CB,
To ask him how far up some skirt can he see.
While ignoring the roadway, four dark, beady eyes,
Are transfixed on a pair of voluptuous thighs.

Then something went snap somewhere deep in his brain,
Some said he was lucid; some said he's insane.
But there in the center lane on the black top,
He put on his brakes and he came to a stop.
He turned off the ignition, then to their dismay,
Put his keys in his pocket and wandered away.
No one knows where he went to or if he's alive.
But he slowed down rush hour on I-95.

*violation of probation

Condo Commandos

∞≈∽

Saul and Esther Feldman tore their roots loose from their slum
And invested their life savings in a condominium.
It was nestled near a great green hill, the highest spot around.
The sunlight sparkled on the lake that drained the swampy ground.

The gate was operated by a small magnetic card.
A prohibition on all pets, so none would foul their yard.
An eight-foot fence of chain link with barbed wire at the top,
Discouraged any trespassers who should decide to stop.

They had a minor set back when one day past their inspection,
Prevailing winds began to blow from a southeasterly direction.
Organic matter festering beneath the tropic sun,
Caused olfactory sensations that would make the sinus run.

Their suspicions were confirmed when they discovered that the hill
Adjacent to their condo was the county owned landfill.
Then gradually they realized the way it operated,
The fence 'round their community kept them incarcerated.

Their warden was the president of their association,
Who constantly was searching for each petty violation.
Like burned out light bulbs on the porch; improperly bagged trash;
A guest parked in a neighbor's spot. He'd collect the fines in cash.

Their sunny dispositions turned into intemperance
When the relative humidities hit ninety plus percents.
Mosquitoes swarmed at sunset, no-see-ems at the dawn.
While hordes of chinch bugs decimated their Bermuda lawn.

The *coup de grâce* descended on a late September day,
When the weatherman informed them that a storm was on the way.

67

The wind screamed like a banshee; rain like Niagra Falls.
The garbage from the landfill gently bobbed inside their walls.

It was then that they decided that they really missed the snow.
And, like Moses out of Egypt, it was time for them to go.
They loaded their belongings and commenced to venture forth,
With the final admonition that, "It's not like this up North!"

Suburban Submersion

Part I

The problem first got started when the corps of engineers,
In an act of self promotion seeking accolades and cheers,
Decided it would dig a ditch across the Sunshine State,
A nice shortcut for boaters and for barges hauling freight.

They started out at Stuart, headed west to Indiantown,
Built a lock at Port Mayaca so the neighbors wouldn't drown.
Across Lake Okeechobee to Moore Haven and La Belle;
They dredged on out past Ft. Myers Beach through rock and sand and shell.

The engineers were mighty proud of their amazing feat,
A waterway from sea to gulf, magnificently neat.
If they knew then what they know now, they would have called a halt,
Before their excavation caused the subterranean fault.

Part II

Like hungry hordes of locusts they invaded from the North
To escape the frigid winters which they all seem to abhorr'th.
On boats and rafts and inner tubes they floated from the South
To escape the bitter tyrannies that they have disavow'th.

Developers drained dismal swamps and built the concrete hives
That would house the interlopers for their desperate, dismal lives.
They also built cliff dwellings overlooking every beach,
So high they blocked the noonday sun; put Heaven within reach.

The weight of all these buildings on the state's southeastern tip
Was causing, imperceptibly, a geologic dip.
The land they pumped and dried, and tried to suck the water out,
While Mother Nature helped with a prolonged, historic drought.

69

Part III

Ernest "Tubby" Turner was a family disgrace.
To say that he was overweight would understate the case.
His belly hung below his knees, his thighs like kegs in girth.
Whenever Tubby took a step, he seemed to shake the earth.

One February evening in two thousand twenty two,
As sleet was beating on the panes he knew what he would do.
He'd head on down to Florida for soaking up some sun,
Which would take a lot of soaking 'cause he weighed a quarter ton.

He traveled down the Interstate that's numbered ninety-five.
Two beefy hands engulfed the wheel as he commenced to drive.
He only stopped to fill the tank and knew he had it made
When he saw the sign announcing, "Welcome to Miami-Dade."

Epilogue

They claimed the land at first began to quiver and to quake,
Soon followed by a trembling and a shudder and a shake.
A creak, a crack, a rumble, then a supersonic boom.
Next, the rushing of the water as the ocean sealed their doom.

The people were hysterical, afraid that they would drown.
They watched in abject terror as their buildings tumbled down.
The populace all perished in their underwater graves,
As this modern day Atlantis slowly slipped beneath the waves.

Although it's hypothetical; no evidence to track;
They think that Tubby was the straw that broke the camel's back.
Before he made his visit, things had teetered on the brink,
But Tubby's weight had tipped the scales and made South Florida sink.

Silver Springs

The roadside's getting tacky so this must be Silver Springs,
A treasured jewel of Florida within concentric rings
Of tourist traps well baited for the bumbling bourgeoisie
Who clamor for cool T-shirts and pink shells plucked from the sea.
The neon sign at Sunny Plaza Motel is obscene
And Chop Stix specializes in Korean (South) cuisine.
The price of the admission for a couple for a day
Explains why there's a pawn shop situated blocks away.
Ninety-nine point eight percent pure water gushes out,
More than half a billion gallons in a day or thereabout,
Creating "Nature's Theme Park" for the reptiles, fish, and birds,
And the hordes of sweaty humans who all congregate in herds.
But, the largest concentration of humanity congests,
To bob around in inner tubes like giant floating nests,
Or plummet down the twisting chutes attempting suicide
At the man made next door theme park with its giant water slide.

Epidermic Epidemic

An epidermic epidemic is pervasive through our land,
From head to toe; from front to back; and even hand to hand;
As living tissues metamorph to rainbow-colored hues.
The cause yet undetermined so we must explore the clues.
Chloroflourocarbons now deplete the ozone layer,
Reducing our protection from the atmospheric air.
When massive slabs of flesh protrude above, below, around,
The skimpy bits of clothing that today seem to abound,
The UV rays of sunlight prompt skin cells to rearrange.
Parboiled in a bath of sweat, there's catalytic change.
Then when the outer layer has been griddled like French crepes,
Chameleon-like it's altered into most fantastic shapes.
So always use some sunscreen, wear a hat, long sleeves, and shoes,
Because there's scientific evidence the sun creates tattoos.

Crustacean Frustration

∽ၑ∾

"Just stop what you're doing and jump in the car.
Haul ass for Palatka, it ain't all that far.
The shrimp are migrating. The moon is just right.
We're filling up buckets all day and all night."
Six short hours later and two tanks of gas,
I'm out on a dock with a net I can't cast.
I'm heaving great handfuls of brownish red clay
And cut rate cat food from the Wal-Mart display,
Mixed up with some fish meal dumped out of a bag.
(A buzzard flew over and started to gag.)
Then we threw some pellets of salt in there, too,
To increase salinity; season the stew.
We turned on the dock lights, the shrimp to attract
And shortly thereafter, mosquitoes attacked.
But now we were ready. Yep, we were all set.
Just stand on the end there and throw out the net.
"First off, tie this rope with a loop to your wrist.
The top in your left hand; fold here but don't twist.
Hold this in your teeth but don't bite on the lead.
Bunch this in your right hand, positioned ahead.
Rotate to your left side, then swing to the right.
Let everything go, most especially your bite,
Or you'll be investing in prosthetic teeth
With implants to hold them in place underneath."
I promptly got humbled, my life at an ebb,
Entangled in mesh like a fly in a web.
But I kept on slinging 'til I got it right
With blisters on fingers and arm muscles tight.
Caught mullet and ladyfish, blue crabs and shad.
We could have made chowder from all that we had.
For some unknown reason, the shrimp did not roam,
And unlike myself, they all stayed safe at home.
My hosts were embarrassed, "Well, what can we say?
What a shame that you couldn't come up yesterday."

Frances and Jeanne

Frances was a harlot and her sister, Jeanne, a whore.
They raped the virgin Treasure Coast, September of '04.
Trees uprooted; roofs ripped off; the power lines all died.
And in the sultry aftermath, our nerves were getting fried.

The gas lines ran for several blocks until the pumps ran dry,
And neighbors fought for sheets of wood, both particle and ply.
Batteries were hoarded; canned goods stockpiled on our shelves,
While we ran around in circles much like Santa's frantic elves.

Our generators roared to life and thundered days and nights,
Refueled from plastic canisters with beams from failing lights,
In the early morning hours when they died from empty tanks.
Mosquito hoards would suck our blood and murmur words of thanks.

Spaghetti-like extension cords snaked twisted on the floor
Just waiting to ensnare a foot. We tripped; we fell; we swore.
Phone lines snapped like sewing thread; the cable next to go.
The only thing still working: our transistor radio.

Our swimming pools became our tubs into which we'd plunge
With shampoo and a bar of soap 'til they turned green with grunge.
Water poured in toilet tanks. We'd flush but once a day.
An indoor outhouse disinfected well with Lysol spray.

Our chainsaws screeched in agony like fingernails on slate,
While ripping through the shattered trunks that we'd eviscerate.
We hauled the amputated limbs by flatbed trailer load
And stacked them at the tree morgue where the driveway meets the road.

We'll have no Christmas tree this year, the first time in our lives,
Because the scent of pine trees has me breaking out in hives,
We'll drink a toast of eggnog and we'll raise a plastic cup,
As we're taking down the shutters when the Christmas lights go up.

Feliz Navidad

The office Christmas party sort of ended in a fog
As I partook of pink champagne and bourboned up eggnog.

I cheerfully assured my boss that I was fine to drive,
Though it was nearly midnight and we'd cranked it up at five.

The center line was wavy. I kept veering to and fro.
The traffic lights looked double and they gave an eerie glow.

Find a designated driver. I must formulate a plan.
'Cause if a cop should stop me, I'll spend Christmas in the can.

Then I got a great idea—it was like a lightening strike,
When I saw a Guatamalan guy out peddling his bike.

"Perdoname, Señor," I said, "but can you drive a car?"
"Muy bueno," he replied. "You want to go how far?"

I really liked his attitude. The little dude had spunk.
So we loaded up his bicycle and put it in the trunk.

Once safely home, I tipped him, then to prove I'm not a slouch,
I insisted that he spend the night and offered him the couch.

When I got up next morning, he and his bike were gone,
Along with several presents and our Santa from the lawn.

He'd left a written message which I thought a little odd.
"¡Muchas gracías, Señor, y muy Feliz Navidad!"

Oriental Ornamentals

All year long the Chinese nation
Spurred by profit motivation
Waited with anticipation
For our Christmas celebration.

Every Chung and every Chang,
Every Woo and every Wang,
Everyone, the whole damn gang,
Cut and stitched and glued and sang:

>"Jinger beers! Jinger beers!
>Jinger otter way!
>Oh, wot phun it is to lide
>In one hose oben sray!"

Working, toiling unabated
Christmas characters created.
Nylon bags will be inflated;
Staked in yards well decorated.

Snowmen, elves, and reindeer play.
Santa's in a full-sized sleigh.
Angels and the Wisemen pray.
Jesus in the manger lay.

With the breaking of the dawn,
The cheerful totems all are gone.
Piles of fabric heaped on lawns,
Like rainbow skins shed by pythons.

Here's the reason. Here's the essence
Of the figures' lost tumescence.
Created with design dehiscence.
Chinese know planned obsolescence.

Loxahatchee Lamentations

∽∾∽

I am the Loxahatchee River. I was scenic, wild, and free.
My feet were in the wetlands and my mouth is in the sea.
My banks were overshadowed by the emerald canopies
Of the cypress that stood stately, thrusting up their knobby knees.
My water's stained to ebony like tea steeped in the sun;
It percolates through fallen leaves and has since time's begun.
The alligators motionless as half-submerging logs,
And panthers slipped along my shores through silent morning fogs.
Blue herons and white egrets stalked my shallows for their prey,
While eagles and the ospreys soared above and screamed dismay.

Your quenchless thirst for water drained my slough and your machines
Have dug canals to irrigate your fairways and your greens.
You ration out my water and control my ebb and flow
By diverting what's my birthright just to make your tax rolls grow.
My beaches you've replaced with walls. They've all been concrete curbed,
Where baitfish hid in mangrove roots and snook prowled undisturbed.
You turned my outlet to an inlet so the salty waters flood
With the tides up tributaries to contaminate my blood.
The cypress trunks stand skeletal like tombstones for their dead,
Where vultures perch and watch and wait; they know what lies ahead.

My ecosystem's fragile and it cannot tolerate
Another land development to which you allocate
The water that, by Nature's Law, is mine and mine alone.
Learn lessons from mistakes you've made and scars that I have shown.
The means and opportunity are both within your grip
To protect me from stagnation and the rivulet's final drip.
Open up your floodgates; put an end to all my strife.
Restore my flow so I'll retain some quality of life.
I am the Loxahatchee River. I was scenic, wild, and free.
I am the Loxahatchee River and I'm yearning to be me.

Vermont

House Guests

The Invitation

We'd love to have you visit if you'd care to take a jaunt
To the lovely Northeast Kingdom in the green state of Vermont.
In the summer we'll go hiking or we'll kayak on some pond.
In the fall we'll watch the colors change with Nature's magic wand.
In the winter we'll go skiing where it's snowing by the ton.
In the spring we'll boil syrup when the sap begins to run.
So come on up and see us any season that we're there.
You'll enjoy Michelle's great cooking and you'll breathe clean country air.

Day One

We'll pick you up in Burlington whenever you arrive.
Don't think a thing about it—it's a nice two hour drive.
We'll come back down tomorrow for the bag the airline lost.
Don't rent a car. It's senseless for you to incur that cost.
You brought your dog! How wonderful! He sleeps right in your beds?
You think he'll be house broken soon? Don't worry if he sheds.
You must be tired from your long trip. The pots and pans can wait.
Just pile your dishes in the sink. We know it's getting late.

Day Two

The weatherman says we'll be blessed with two more days of rain.
The farmers claim we need it, but it really is a pain.
The dirt and rocks you're tracking in will scratch the hardwood floor.
Remove your shoes when you come in. That's what the mud room's for.
You seem to play Monopoly for keeps, like Donald Trump;
And after several hours when you'd clearly kicked my rump,
I thought your celebration was a trifle overdone
'Til I learned we'd played for money when I thought we'd played for fun.

Day Three

I choked on hot, black coffee and I doubted I'd survive
When your daughters and their boyfriends pulled up, waving, in our drive.
Michelle became hysterical and I was looking grave,
As we recalled the admonition wise Ben Franklin gave
Of odors which will emanate from house guests and from fish.
Which we would both eliminate if we had but one wish.
So if we get to drinking and insist that you should stay,
Remember we don't mean it and please hurry on your way.

For Sale

"New home. Three wooded acres with maples and white birch.
Breathtaking views from every room. This one concludes your search!
Four bedrooms, three full bathrooms. Enclosed two-car garage.
A stone fireplace and chimney grace this most impressive lodge.
All counter tops are granite. The roof is standing seam.
With rough-cut cedar siding, this house is just a dream.
This one's such a bargain! The owners say they'll swap,
For a single room log cabin on secluded mountain top."

Bill and Jack

They were Vermont bred
From tail end to head
One full ton of muscle and bone.
Their hooves big as plates,
Fresh shod with iron weights,
Rang out like a hammer on stone.

Their withers head high,
Necks arched toward the sky,
Hindquarters as solid as oak.
Their coats dappled gray;
They pulled sled or sleigh
With spirit that couldn't be broke.

That Saturday night
They were in for the fight
Of their lives at the Barton State fair.
And each of the teams
Was driven by dreams:
Becoming the champion pair.

In round after round,
Hooves gouging the ground,
They strained at their harness and tack.
Together they lunged,
They heaved and they plunged,
'Til the driver yelled, "Whoa, Bill and Jack!"

Just past twelve o'clock
They placed the last block
Of cement on the battered old sled.
Their sweat turned to steam

As team after team
Failed and from the arena was led.

The dust made a haze
As the two dappled grays
Backed up and were hooked to the weight.
With flicks of the reins
They pulled like two trains
Of box cars full loaded with freight.

They looked good as gold
And loud thunder rolled,
As they staggered off for the wire.
The blood ran bright red
As their nostrils bled.
Their bright eyes were blazing with fire.

They pricked up their ears
To the roars and the cheers,
Then Jack looked at Bill with a smirk,
"I can't speak for you,
But now that we're through,
I'm finding a new line of work."

Effie's Barn

With granite blocks and poured cement, they formed the barn's foundation,
Before the Great Depression cast its pall across the nation.
The hardwood skeleton framed out with hand cut posts and beams,
Hauled from the woodlot hitched behind the massive Belgian teams.

Each clapboard fastened to the frame with hammer driven nails.
The barnyard well surrounded by a fence of hand split rails.
Planked hayloft floor and silo stored a winter's worth of feed.
Tin roofed, white washed, red painted in accordance with the creed.

As season turned to season and year turned into year,
The barn stood stout and sturdy and from deep within you'd hear
The creaking of the wagon wheels while hauling in the bales;
The lowing of the milk cows and the clatter of the pails.

The Farmall hauled manure from the reeking bowels below
And spread it on the pastures when the grass began to grow.
The barn housed all the livestock and kept them safe from harm.
It was the very heart and soul of every working farm.

But now the roof is sagging on its old, arthritic spine.
A sinking ship that's listing well above her water line.
The cobwebs coat the rafters like gray skeins of woolen yarn,
And only starlings occupy the stalls in Effie's barn.

The engineers and builders couldn't justify the cost
To attempt a restoration of a building that was lost.
The Vermont farmer's daughter then dismissed them with a frown,
"I'll go broke to shore it up before I'll tear it down."

The tired foundation buttressed like the walls of Notre Dame;
The broken posts replaced with new to straighten up the frame.
The beams jacked up and lifted; the walls cross-cabled tight.
The faded clapboards painted red; the window frames in white.

Old wood spoked wheels with iron rims are leaned against the walls,
And hay rakes rest on battered boards within the empty stalls.
But close your eyes and listen. You'll hear the cowbells chime
And you'll see the Holsteins headed for the barn at milking time.

Mootlers

If tramping around in the woods you desire
To warm your phalanges with help from a fire,
Insuring ignition's unlikely enough
Until you've assembled all manner of stuff.
I'll later explain why, but trust me for now.
You won't understand so don't furrow your brow.
But first you must locate a moose antler shed,
That paddley thing from a bull moose's head.
It may take some hours of stomping around
With both eyes transfixed on the snow covered ground.
(And just a suggestion when planning your route,
Be sure you're in woods where some bull moose hang out.)
The next thing you'll need is fresh pitch from a pine
Or bark from a birch will most likely work fine.
You might want to scour your pockets for lint
If all you've brought with you is steel and a flint.
(But having tried that way when you were a Scout,
You brought your Bic lighter when you ventured out.)
Now, gather up twigs that are brittle and dead,
Then sticks and small branches that hang overhead.
And finally limbs that have broken and fell—
You're set to ignite the inferno from Hell.
First stamp down the snow 'til it's hard and compact.
Pile pine pitch and birch bark. Twigs carefully stacked
On top of the tinder will feed the small flame;
Which promptly dies out to your horror and shame.
When, after an hour, your spirit is broke
And all you've produced is a pale wisp of smoke,
You swallow your pride and retrieve from your kit
The fluid for lighting your barbeque pit.
You pile on more wood with the flames leaping higher
Until you've constructed a funeral pyre.
Now cut from a sapling some sticks with forked ends

And sharpen the points so the frankfurter tends
To stay there impaled while you wave it around.
You won't want to eat one if it hits the ground.
The hotdogs once blackened and coated with ash
Are slathered with mustard, consumed with panache.
Now gorged, you are ready to call it a day,
The flames though are roaring and popping away.
A vision of Smokey the Bear fills your head:
A smoldering forest, small creatures lie dead . . .
Remember the "mootler" you first had to find?
I'll bet you'd forgotten. It slipped from your mind.
Well, this is the moment! Yes, this is your ace!
One hand on a brow tine, one hand on the base,
The palmated end works to shovel the snow,
Until you've extinguished the last embers' glow.
Sometimes when you're leaving, if you will look back,
You might see a bull moose who's missing his rack.
You know he's been watching and sometimes I think,
He gives you a great big, old, bull moosey wink.

Aging

When I Grew Up

When grownups used to smile at me
And ask what did I want to be
When I grew up?
The president of all the land,
Or else a cowboy tall and tanned.
That was the life that I had planned.

When my parents would inquire
As to what I did aspire
When I grew up?
I'd tell them that I didn't know,
A doctor, lawyer, CEO?
Then they'd be proud and all aglow.

But secretly I knew I planned
To have a country western band
When I grew up.
I'd sing sad songs of broken hearts
Smash hits would top the Billboard charts.
I'd tour the world's most distant parts.

With pretty girls, I'd have my choice.
I'd pick them up in my Rolls Royce,
When I grew up.
I'd have my mansion on the hill.
My yacht would cost a cool ten mil.
Have cash to burn and time to kill.

For thirty years I've worked the line
Assembled cars that gleam and shine,
When I grew up.
But all I've got for all I've tried,

My pickup and our double-wide;
My ego bruised and wounded pride.

But when I look into your eyes,
I know I won life's grandest prize,
When I grew up.
Those other things can all be damned,
'Cause when I sit and hold your hand,
My life is better than I planned.

The All American Male

We was watchin' TV
The old lady and me,
Eatin' pizza and drinkin' Bud Lite.
We watched it from seven
'Til almost eleven.
We was havin' one helluva night.
Them commercials they run
Are just so much fun;
It was like they was talkin' 'bout me.
And it come to me then,
I was just like them men
And that is a guarandamntee.
My cholesterol'd rise
Thanks to Super Size fries
'Til I got some of that Lipitor.
If I'da used Listerine,
I'da kept my teeth clean.
Them dentures sure make my gums sore.
So I tried Fixodent,
That stuff's like cement.
I can gnaw on pork ribs like a bear.
My heart burn's set free
Thanks to Pepcid AC.
Now I wish I'd quit losin' my hair.
They promised Rogaine
Would fill out my mane
But it only grew hair on my rear.
My pickup's a Dodge,
Which I drive to the Lodge
Whenever I need me a beer.
May God bless the soul
Of Senator Dole
Who's told us without no compunction

That he, like us all,
The great and the small,
Can suffer erectile dysfunction.
Now, pauper or King,
That just ain't a thing
You share with the boys at the bar.
But, thanks to Viagra
The wife, she won't nag ya,
'Cause you can perform like a star.

The Tigress

When women's lib hits menopause,
The tigress sharpens up her claws.
She bides her time and lies in wait,
Her partner to emasculate.
She hears his footsteps on the floor;
He opens up the freezer door.
The ice cubes make a gentle splash,
Into a glass of sour mash.
He sinks into his leather throne,
His lungs emit a tired groan.
From her bedroom lair she senses,
That he's shed his last defenses.
She stalks her prey and with her spring,
His serenity has taken wing.
The stillness shattered by her roars,
She rages at what she abhors:
Her thermostat runs hot and cold.
She mourns her youth, she thinks she's old.
Her body aches. It's not neurosis.
She's getting osteoporosis.
Her life's just heartache and travail.
She's living proof that God's a male.
Throughout her vitriolic rants,
Her mate sits still, like in a trance.
He then inquires with a grin,
"Did you forget your Premarin?"

The Perfect Couple

He had his hair transplanted from
His sidewalls to his dome,
By a specialist who did it in the
Comfort of his home.
When it was wet, he blew it dry
With just a touch of gel.
His roots were colored twice a month
No one could ever tell.

Her appointment at the beauty shop on
Friday's etched in stone.
She has her hair highlighted to a
Natural sun-streaked tone.
Her eyebrows plucked; her face
Massaged; acrylic nails applied.
The staff gives her ovations and
Cannot contain its pride.

He had his eyelids lifted and the
Skin beneath his jowl
Was tightened with such tension
That he couldn't even scowl.
His teeth were crowned and whitened
Like the mountains capped with snow.
The tinted contact lenses gave his
Eyes an azure glow.

The miracles of medicine bestowed
Upon her face
Had ironed out every wrinkle, every
Blemish was erased.
Her eyes were shaped like almonds;
Nose with elevated tip.

96

The collagen injections caused her
Pouting lower lip.

His pectoralis muscles bulged with
Help from silicone
And his liposuctioned abdomen was
Flat as polished stone.
His remake was completed on that great
Day that he chanced,
To learn of the operation that
Would make his thing enhanced.

She had her breasts augmented to
The size of cantaloupes.
They really were spectacular, beyond
Her wildest hopes.
Her thighs and buttocks sculpted
To a size that was petite.
Then she had her bunions straightened
To correct her crooked feet.

They were now the perfect couple
And they knew they had it all.
To confirm it they put mirrors
In their home from wall to wall.
Everywhere they looked they could
Admire their own reflections,
And rejoice that their appearance
Was devoid of imperfections.

But they were devastated when their
Less than perfect friends
Would reject their invitations and
Would never make amends.
Among themselves the friends
Confessed that they were rather bored
And they felt the perfect couple was
A trifle self-absorbed.

So he and she decided that they
Should consult a shrink,
Who pondered while he scratched his
Beard then said, "Here's what I think.
You are the perfect couple; your
Physiques are quite artistic.
My working diagnosis is you might
Be narcissistic."

Designer Jeans

My wife asked me to go with her one day to buy some jeans.
I suggested that she order them on line from L.L. Bean's;
Or else we'd drive my pickup to the Western Tack and Feed.
When I want clothes they always seem to have just what I need.
She kind of smirked and said unless I'm looking for a brawl,
I'd best get in her Cadillac and head it for the mall.
Then after spending hours on a shopping marathon,
I learned to buy designer jeans, you've got to try them on.
She started at Old Navy with some pants pulled off the rack,
But her buttocks bounced around like gophers fighting in a sack.
Went through their stock at Macy's and at Abercrombie's, too.
She must have tried a hundred pairs at Saks Fifth Avenue.
She'd interrogate the sales staff, asking them to scrutinize
And tell her if she'd camouflaged the thickness of her thighs.
Every make and model seemed to make her butt look big;
Compared herself in profile to some fat potbellied pig.
But then in desperation at a boutique called "Eileen's,"
It was like you'd gone to Mecca if you want designer jeans.
There were high rise; there were low rise; they were tapered; they were flared.
Faded, torn, and tattered like they'd need to be repaired.
Double stitched and riveted; embroidered and engraved.
She began to hyperventilate like she'd become depraved.
As she began to try them on, she chortled like a loon;
A butterfly attempting to re-enter its cocoon.
She tugged and pulled and twisted. Her body she'd contort,
Until at last I heard her voice triumphantly report,
"My God! They are a perfect fit! My legs look like string beans!
My buns as elevated as they were back in my teens!"
They cost about three hundred bucks, but they were almost free
Compared to what I might have paid for plastic surgery.

Botox Rocks

With endless ticks, redundant tocks
Our graceless biologic clocks
Transfigure youth with mirthless mocks
Which, mirrored, render aftershocks.
What woes escaped Pandora's box
Compare with footprints left by flocks
Of crows? Beneath the graying locks
Where wrinkles roll like waves on rocks,
Rare opportunity that knocks:
From haggard hag, refurbished fox;
 When needle point injects botox
And muscles sag like droopy sox,
Erasing lines and pits and pocks.

Independence

They both look well past eighty and they're sitting still as stone.
They're traveling together, but they're traveling alone.
My seat is right beside his and he gives the slightest nod
To acknowledge my existence but he doesn't mean to prod.
Although his collar's buttoned, it hangs loosely at his throat.
His tie is neatly knotted and he wears a woolen coat.
His skin stretched taught as tenting from his cheek bones to his chin.
His hands are gnarled and knotty; his chest concave and thin.
She sits and reads a paperback although the lights are dim.
I turn her lamp on overhead by reaching over him.
I smile and say, "I didn't want to see you hurt your eyes."
She tells me that her eyes are fine. I make no more replies.
And for the next two hours, whene'er I sneak a look,
His eyes are staring straight ahead and hers are on her book.
I want to ask him questions but I don't want to intrude,
As he sits there like a statue in his quiet solitude.
I wonder where they're going and about their future plans,
And the lives they've spent together as they sit there holding hands.

The Octogenarian

෧෧෧

When he turned three score years and ten, his life had been waylaid.
He needed reading glasses and a sonic hearing aid.
The pension he'd been promised barely kept food on his plate.
His stock and bond portfolio was shrinking as of late.
He worried that his assets would be gone before he died,
Then they'd stick him in a nursing home and strip him of his pride.
While moaning that his osteoarthritis caused him pain,
He noticed that the room would empty whene'er he'd complain.
Not one soul wanted his advice; in fact, it went ignored.
And rather than enlightened, the recipients got bored.
He felt he was a has-been who'd been had by all his dreams,
As he battled his frustrations and suppressed his silent screams.
Sequentially, the years slipped by until a decade passed;
A gradual awakening when he perceived at last:

Your life begins at eighty if your ticker's ticking well,
And if your other body parts have not all gone to Hell.
The general perception is surprise you're here at all.
The ones who once ignored you, now are at your beck and call.
With every indiscretion, you're eccentric; they're amused.
There never will be one request that you will have refused.
Every word you utter is considered wise and sage.
Mock skepticism clouds each face when you relate your age.
You recognize most faces though you're hazy on the name,
But friends cannot remember yours so no one takes the blame.
If people ask if you've regrets, you tell them, "Mighty few.
They aren't about the things I did. It's what I didn't do."
Now every day's your birthday once you've reached the four score mark.
So fire up all your candles. Don't just sit there in the dark!

Fish Oil

When he turned fifty years of age, he made a solemn vow,
"I will not ingest anything that used to be a cow.
I'll never more partake of pork. No flesh that once drew breath.
By abstinence I'll prolong life and thus forestall my death."

Granola, grains, and vegetables, especially leafy greens;
Frijoles negros, lima, pinto, and navy beans.
Tomatoes, peas, and carrots; eggplant and wild mushrooms;
Potatoes, baked or boiled, and various legumes.

He loaded up on supplements, a truly vast array.
With tablespoons, powders, and pills, he'd start and end each day.
An alphabet of vitamins, enzymes, a probiotic.
His wife believed he was obsessed and just a bit neurotic.

She found him at the table with his head laid on his arm.
She first thought he was sleeping, then reacted with alarm
When she saw he wasn't breathing and his face was bluish gray.
The medical examiner found why he'd passed away.

Lodged within his trachea, (or wind pipe if you will),
An elongated, capsular, gelatinous type pill.
By chemical analysis, a substance somewhat odd:
It was oil from the liver of a North Atlantic cod.

Places

Silent Solitude

∽◟◞∽

While sitting on a fallen tree one afternoon in Maine
I heard a sound I'd never heard; a sound I can't explain.
The air stood still and held its breath. There wasn't any breeze,
To rustle dead leaves on their limbs or rattle tops of trees.

No water tumbling over stones or lapping on some shore.
No waterfalls, no pounding surf or hydrosonic roar.
Tomorrow's rivers hug the firs and insulate the ground,
As more flakes drift down lazily and settle all around.

Not one squirrel barked. No raucous cry from raven, jay, or crow.
No rumble from the clouds above that watched me down below.
The mountains loomed around me and round rocks like headstones stood.
It seemed both time and life stayed still in that great northern wood.

No man sound even dared encroach to violate the calm.
No voice to sing a melody or to recite a psalm.
No airplanes thundered through the sky. I heard no engine drone.
No horns, no bells, no power saws, no ringing telephone.

Until that day I didn't know that noise could disappear,
Or understand those absent sounds that only deaf men hear.
Freed from chaotic clamor for one fleeting interlude,
I whiled away the afternoon in silent solitude.

The Rack and Quack

There's a little old joint by the railroad track,
That folks around here call The Rack and Quack.
The "Rack's" named after the horns on the buck;
That white tail deer that they got stuck
Up over the bar.

The "Quack" is the sound that the mallard drake,
When he was alive, would always make.
'Til he got shot while on the fly
And then got stuffed and set there by,
The pickled egg jar.

There ain't no windows 'cause they all got broke,
That Saturday night when Red told the joke,
About Virgil's wife and the preacher man.
Then the place got rowdy and out of hand,
They all went too far.

The bar's formica and the beer and the wine,
Are advertised on a neon sign,
That flickers and hums through the smoke and the haze.
They say they're gonna fix it here one of these days.
Well, they say they are.

The parking lot's full of deep pot holes,
But that don't bother the poor lost souls,
In their pickup trucks with the four wheel drive,
Who wouldn't be caught there dead or alive,
In a normal car.

There's a juke box standing by the screen back door,
And there's peanut shells on the plywood floor.
The beer's on tap and the wine's from a jug,

That the women sip and the men all chug,
From a mason jar.

There's one bathroom at the end of the hall,
It's a single seater and there ain't no stall.
So when the line's too long and you got to go,
Seems some folks head outside, you know,
Out under the stars.

They won't accept Visa or American Express,
Which is why, they suspect, that the I.R.S.,
And the C.I.A. and the F.B.I.,
Conduct their surveillance with a watchful eye.
But from afar.

A color TV used to hang on the wall,
'Til late one night in a free for all,
A construction worker who's a former marine,
Threw his cue at some actor up there on the screen.
It was like a war.

The roof's caved in, the paint's starting to peel.
They don't serve hard liquor and you can't get a meal.
But the locals all love it and keep coming back,
'Cause there's no place else like The Rack and Quack.
The neighborhood bar.

Sheepless Days and Darkless Nights

We paid to have fun
In the land where the sun
Won't set on the range called The Brooks.
The price that you pay
You must learn the hard way
And not in some tourist guide books.

We shouldered our packs;
Sixty pounds on our backs;
A rifle, a stick, and a prayer.
The golden horned sheep
Thrive up there where it's steep
With notable absence of air.

On tundra we sunk
To our knees in green gunk
That grew on the hard permafrost.
Extracting our feet,
Every step a repeat.
Move onward whatever the cost.

The Lord's name in vain
We uttered profane
On talus slopes covered with shale.
Where one careless stride
Would commence a landslide,
And they'd carry you out in a pail.

We forded the streams,
Suppressing our screams,
Where ice water roared down the falls.

We cautiously tread
Over rocks in the bed
Like oily, gray bowling balls.

The soles of my feet
Were like putrified meat
Marinating in poly-wool blend.
Aromas obscene
Would waft out between
Boot laces from toe to top end.

A high glacier hung
From a peak like a tongue
Of ice that was wrinkled and blue.
On higher we'd climb
Until after sometime,
My tongue also hung out askew.

It never got dark
As the sun made an arc
At latitude sixty-nine North.
No East and no West,
Where the sun's rise and rest,
Could guide us as we ventured forth.

Each evening we camped
Inside tents that were cramped
As if we were back in the womb.
In mummy bags wrapped,
Where we slept and we napped,
Like Pharaohs in some ancient tomb.

Each day we would glass
For Dall sheep eating grass
High up on the slopes in a cloud.
But ewes with their lambs,
And three quarter curl rams
Were all we could see through the shroud.

We lost several days
While tent bound in a craze,
Weathered in by the fog, rain, and snow.
A nylon cocoon,
Where both midnight and noon
Look the same and there's no place to go.

But then one clear day
A large trophy ram lay
Overlooking our camp on a ledge.
A three-hour sneak
To the top of a peak
That finally gave us the edge.

There just was no way
To get closer that day
So Bill had to play out his cards.
With one trigger squeeze,
The ram fell to his knees,
At four hundred eighty-eight yards!

We made our escape
With the meat, horns, and cape
Secured to their packs with a lash.
My final disgrace
As we left that damned place?
I packed out the week's worth of trash.

Greasy Slough

Snared with nets in a lost lagoon,
Or pothole out near Saskatoon.
A metal band with numbers stamped
Upon each orange leg was clamped
But when released, his wings beat free.
Long summer season's feeding spree
Gave way to fall. The north winds blew.
Fly south! Fly south to Greasy Slough.

Into the flooded timber maze,
Through water slick with skim ice glaze.
No sooner were the decoys spread
Than angel wings flapped overhead.
In opposition, moon and sun;
Night was ended, day begun,
As waterfowl in dark clouds flew
Out of the rice toward Greasy Slough.

Wings alternating dark then white,
Pulse fast like blinking strings of light.
A duck call rasps a pleading sound.
They turn and bank, then come around;
Circling lower; wings cupped and set.
They don't suspect deception yet.
Heads green with iridescent hue,
Final approach to Greasy Slough.

Three shotguns thundered. Mallards crashed.
Still waters geysered where they splashed.
Expertly fetched by old Sambeau,
With dripping coat of calico.

The final drake, limits in hand,
Around each leg, a metal band.
For fifteen hundred miles he flew
To meet his fate at Greasy Slough.

Yellow Pine

Seems some folks took to drinking when they closed the Stibnite Mine,
And there ain't no AA meetings in the town of Yellow Pine.
There's just one lodge; one general store; The Corner Bar saloon,
Which closes down at two A.M. and opens up by noon.

Mike is missing several teeth, but that ain't no disgrace.
He lost them when he missed the ring and landed on his face.
So he decided to retire and dropped out of the game.
Mike shoots his pistols, drinking beer, which helps improve his aim.

Indian Bob fought Viet Cong. Three tours is what they say.
He got his scars in battle and he earned the Green Beret.
Now vodka helps him ease his pain. His pistol's in his rack.
You couldn't find a better man than Bob to watch your back.

Don's a modern mountain man who heads out with his string
Into the high back country when the winter turns to spring.
He makes his living off the land; sleeps out beneath the moon,
But when Don rides back into town, he'll hit the first saloon.

The residents are sturdy stock who best are left alone.
They take whatever comes their way and never piss and moan.
So don't go try to change them. They all think they're doing fine.
And there ain't no AA meetings in the town of Yellow Pine.

Santa Cruise

On our cruise ship to Alaska headed northward toward the Pole
Were twenty Santaholics all committed to their role.
Full tangled beards of white and gray adorned each chubby face,
While snowy locks of thinning hair were wafting out in space.
Great bulbous, veiny noses hung beneath small beady eyes,
While yellowed teeth clenched pipe stems from which clouds of smoke arise.
Like rotund candied apples, each one adorned in reds,
From high-topped canvas sneakers to bandanas on their heads.
Bermuda shorts with knee socks; some full bib overalls;
Suspenders sporting blinking lights bedecked their pelvic walls.
In cardinal, carmine, claret; in ruby, poppy, scarlet;
In crimson, lobster, strawberry; they outshone any harlot.
Each one had a gimmick or performed some magic trick
He'd utilize to emphasize his corny Santa schtick.
What really was amazing was the food they'd put away
At the breakfast, lunch, and dinner, and the late midnight buffet.
But my favorite jolly Santa sat alone sprawled in a chair,
Ignoring hanging glaciers with a fixed and vacant stare.
No kids were climbing on his lap demanding loads of toys.
He didn't have to ask if they had been good girls and boys.
He didn't have to worry about spreading Christmas cheer.
He sat in silence sipping on a cold six pack of beer.

Relationships

PICKER FIXER

❧

The first time that she married was the apex of her dreams.
She said, "Don't worry, Momma, 'cause he ain't like what he seems.
He'll drink a little whiskey 'cause it helps him to unwind.
It enables him to open up and say what's on his mind.
There's only been a couple times he's passed out in the yard;
And I know he's hit me, Momma, but he's never hit me hard."
She's got to fix her picker. It's as broken as it gets.
And with her picker broken she'll have nothing but regrets.

The second time she married she could thank her lucky stars
That her man would never frequent any honky tonks or bars.
He'd play a little poker, shoot some craps, and spin roulette.
On horses, dogs, and football games he'd maybe place a bet.
Tomorrow he'd be winning—an ace was in his boot.
But when she finally left him, he had left her destitute.
She's got to fix her picker. It's as broken as it gets.
And with her picker broken she'll have nothing but regrets.

The third time that she married would conclude a lengthy search
Of tabernacles, synagogues, and every type of church.
He wouldn't drink or gamble and he didn't smoke or chew.
He'd appreciate a woman's form when she was passing through.
It didn't hurt if he would flirt and be a little fresh.
But what she couldn't take was his partaking of the flesh.
She's got to fix her picker. It's as broken as it gets.
And with her picker broken she'll have nothing but regrets.

She started contemplating what was wrong with all her men,
And with some introspection, well, it all came to her then.
She couldn't fix their defects, though the Good Lord knew she'd tried,
And when each marriage ended something deep inside her died.
To love herself completely was the essence of her plan.

Until she picked herself up first, she couldn't pick a man.
She's got to fix her picker. It's as broken as it gets.
And with her picker broken she'll have nothing but regrets.

The Latest Husband

This here's my latest husband. I swear he's the best one yet.
Them other ones I traded in and I've got no regret.
Their warranties were limited, excluded wear and tear.
Their guarantees inflated like balloons blown up with air.
As each one got road weary and would start to fall apart,
A newer model pulled right up which was state of the art.
This one's still got all his teeth, a nice full head of hair,
He's got no body piercings, and no tattoos anywhere.
He hasn't had a felony conviction in his life
And he don't pay alimony to some bitchy former wife.
He gets a steady paycheck that he cashes Friday night
Then he brings me home a cold six pack of bottled Miller Lite.
Right now there ain't a single thing I know he's doing wrong,
So I guess I'll stick with this one 'til an upgrade comes along.

Forever and Then Some

We first said, "I love you," while still in our teens.
We had no idea what "I love you" means.
An ache in my chest from your kiss on my cheek;
The touch of your hand would make my knees grow weak.
I could not explain where these feelings came from.
I'll love you forever and ever and then some.

We both worked together fulfilling our dream,
Through good times and bad times we pulled as a team.
We cared for each other in sickness and health.
We never got rich but our love was our wealth.
Thoughts of life without you make my mind go numb.
I'll love you forever and ever and then some.

Throughout our whole lifetime we're joined at the heart.
They'll both beat together 'til death do us part.
No one here on earth can know what happens then,
But I've given my promise again and again,
That we'll be together what Kingdom may come.
I'll love you forever and ever and then some.

Amour Allure

Two lovers lounge on Pfeiffer Beach,
While setting sun tints salt spray peach.
High soaring seagulls cry and screech,
Seek morsels hiding underneath
The floating kelp, a seaweed wreath.
Hard pounding waves give no relief.
Their waters stream like tears of grief
Down rocky faces void of speech.
He felt his passion rise beneath,
Then pursed his lips. She flossed her teeth.

Bipolar High Rollers

Bipolar high rollers is what that couple is.
Depressive parts are all on her. The manic parts are his.
His clouds are lined with silver; hers all are trimmed in black.
He skips through fields of daisies; she trips over every crack.
He's cheerful and he's chubby, maybe just a tad obese.
She's completely anorexic and she looks about deceased.
His glass is always almost full while hers is almost gone.
He's king in this chess game of life; she's but a lowly pawn.
They've both tried medication but it didn't do much good.
He got more hyperactive; she, more misunderstood.
But they are bound together. Each to the other clings.
He says, "She is my anchor." She says, "He is my wings."

Calloused Heart

∽◡∾

You've got more callous on your heart
than I've got on my hands.
You strive to drive our lives apart
and wreck our future plans.

The callous on your heart is growing
thicker day by day.
The stuff gets rougher, tougher, girl
the longer you're away.

I'm here at home with our eight kids,
still working six to four.
I heed and feed and plead with them
since you walked out our door.

You're prob'ly soaking up the sun
in some exotic clime.
With booze you choose to lose my dear
your former life sublime.

I'd love to have you back again
and try a brand new start.
I'll slave and save to shave away,
the callous from your heart.

The Other Cheek

When he was just a little boy, he went to Sunday school,
And there the teacher taught them to obey The Golden Rule.
"Always do to others what you'd have them do to you."
Let that be your motto and your guide your whole life through.
Blessed are those that keep the peace for Jesus loves the meek.
You must forgive your enemies and turn the other cheek.
Always forgive your enemies and turn the other cheek.

When he had children of his own he taught them not to fight
And to ask to learn forgiveness when they said their prayers at night.
He wanted them to know it's best to love your fellow man,
And even one small, senseless act can soon get out of hand.
When it gets down and dirty and you're really up the creek,
Just take a breath then walk away and turn the other cheek.
Just take a breath then walk away and turn the other cheek.

She served the legal papers on him asking for divorce.
She wanted alimony and the house and kids, of course.
She left the bills for him to pay and asked for child support,
And said unless he'd stipulate, she'd haul him off to court.
He knew about forgiveness and those things the churches teach,
But sometimes it is difficult to practice what you preach.
He felt like he was sinking in a rowboat full of leaks,
And that's when he advised her she could kiss his other cheeks.

Thy Codependent Valentine

Come lean on me and I'll be thine;
Thy codependent Valentine.
Thine every wish is my command.
I'll wait upon thee foot and hand.
(Or hand and foot, should thou prefer.)
What e'er thou sayest, I concur.
Where e'er thou goest, I shall go.
I'll bring thee joy; dispel thy woe.
What thou desireth, I'll provide.
What thou commandeth, I'll abide.
Thou art my reason now to live.
My very life to thee I give.
Thou art my passion and my dream.
To thee I yield my self esteem.

No Wife, No Kids, No Dog

When he turned twenty-seven he had lost the urge to roam.
He was happy living single in his pre-owned, prefab home.
But after cogitating on the mysteries of life,
His world would have more meaning if he found a loving wife.
He went and placed a want ad in The Personal Gazette,
"Single, straight, hard-working male. Completely out of debt.
I'll make some woman happy, like a feed trough makes a hog.
I'm ready for a family: a wife, some kids, a dog."

When he turned thirty-seven he'd achieved his wildest dreams.
His solitude disrupted by the piercing shrieks and screams
Of his precious little offspring as they'd frolic, fight, and play
In the house that had the mortgage that he knew he'd never pay.
They joined the local country club; his wife, the Junior League.
The PTA and T-ball games provided life's intrigue.
The years all ran together in a hazy, swirling fog
Of events entirely focused on his wife, his kids, the dog.

When he turned forty-seven his receding hair was thin.
Beneath his granite jaw there hung a flabby extra chin.
His wife was having flashes and her hips were getting wide,
But she waged a valiant battle as she fought to save her pride.
His kids were busy smoking dope and drinking underage.
He felt about as worthless as a lion in a cage.
His only conversations were an endless monologue
That largely went unanswered by his wife, his kids, the dog.

When he turned fifty-seven he was swigging through the foam
Of a six pack in the comfort of his pre-owned, prefab home.
His wife decided she had needs that he could not fulfill,
And left in search of happiness beyond some emerald hill.

His children finally moved away and struck out on their own.
The dog departed also after choking on a bone.
He sat there smiling simply like a bump upon some log.
A state of pure serenity: no wife, no kids, no dog.

The Eulogy

"I am a very simple man
For work, I drive a truck.
I've tried to do the best I can
When I've run low on luck.
I'll tell you now, my heart is broke."
He shook and heaved a sigh.
He tried to speak but with a choke
The man began to cry.
"I know it ain't the Christian thing
But, damn, I'm mad at God!
I know that being mad won't bring
Her back. Now ain't it odd?
We spend so much to make the guns,
The bombs, and things that kill.
Why can't we be instead the ones
To find the magic pill
To cure the cancer that my wife
Had battled seven years?
You see it finally took her life
And left me just these tears."

The Center of the Circle

In the center of the circle, they were seated face-to-face.
His head hung with dejection. Overcome by his disgrace,
He whispered, "I'm so sorry that I've hurt you. Can't you please,
Forgive me? I'm an addict and I have a dread disease.
Prescription drugs and alcohol destroyed my self-esteem.
I'm existing in a hazy world; a fogged, confusing dream.
I know that I have lost your trust. I know that I'm to blame.
But, I've got to turn it over. I can't live with all this shame."

In the center of the circle, she was staring in his eyes.
"I knew that I could fix you, but then much to my surprise,
When everything was perfect and I had you in control,
My trappings of convention were like bondage of your soul.
The carnage of rebellion would lie scattered on the floor.
Judgmental and resentful, I would bail you out once more.
We each fueled our infernos; danced with demons 'round the blaze.
We had no stars to guide us, while we wandered through the maze."

In the center of the circle, they had no defense or shield.
Each one could only listen while raw feelings were revealed.
No quarter or compassion; no surrender or retreat;
Just honest words that tumbled forth; no lying or deceit.
And then they sat in silence as the world around them wheeled.
In awe as true serenity began to be revealed.
Accepting what they could not change and letting things just be;
With courage just to change themselves, they'd set each other free.

Believin'

～ ❧ ～

When I woke up this mornin', I was feelin' kinda sad.
My life had took a down beat; everthing was breakin' bad.
My best friend died a month ago; girlfriend's at Betty Ford.
Huntin' season's over now. What else could go wrong, Lord?
My shakin' hand was startin' to unscrew the plastic top
From a quart of Black Jack Daniels, when there's something made me stop.
I started makin' up a list of things I'm thankful for,
Then stuck it up with magnets on the 'frigerator door.
The child support and alimony's both paid up to date.
I've got until the fifteenth 'fore the rent's considered late.
The car ain't leakin' oil and the tires still got some tread,
And lookin' in the mirror, it don't look much like I'm dead.
I ain't got cancer, heart disease, or clap near as I know.
I can live with this lumbago and the gout's in just one toe.
There ain't a single kid in jail or doin' drugs today.
The last one's off probation come the thirtieth of May.
The dog got cured of heartworms and we're gainin' on the mange.
There's still two burners workin' on the Sears electric range.
The toilet's workin' perfect since we pumped the septic tank.
I retrieved the outboard motor when my boat capsized and sank.
I bought five Lotto tickets 'cause the jackpot's twenty mil.
I've never won a dollar, but I know someday I will.
You've got to keep believin' everything will turn out right,
And be thankful that you're livin' when you go to sleep at night.

My Wife Threw Out My Underwear

My wife threw out my underwear,
My very special, favorite pair.
One day she just declared them old.
Gave them the pitch and not the fold.
They were boxers, once bright white.
Elastic waistband not too tight.
No buttons on the frontal fly.
No snaps to snap, no strings to tie.
Made by Jockey. Loved by me.
Vintage 1993.
Those underwear had seen it all.
They'd had a blast. They'd had a ball.
I'd worn them out on our first date.
They'd been up early. Got home late.
They'd been to Banff and Lake Louise.
Been out on boats, downhill on skis.
They rode a horse in Idaho.
They'd been in ten degrees below.
They'd gone to church. They'd gone to court.
To Maine at some seaside resort.
They'd been up to Alaska twice.
They'd hiked up mountains, fell on ice.
They'd hunted elk and ducks and deer.
They'd had a wonderful career.
I would have felt like such a lout,
That night I took the garbage out,
If I had known my wife would dare
To throw away my underwear.

Made in the USA
Charleston, SC
12 February 2012